TULSA CITY-COUNTY LIBRARY

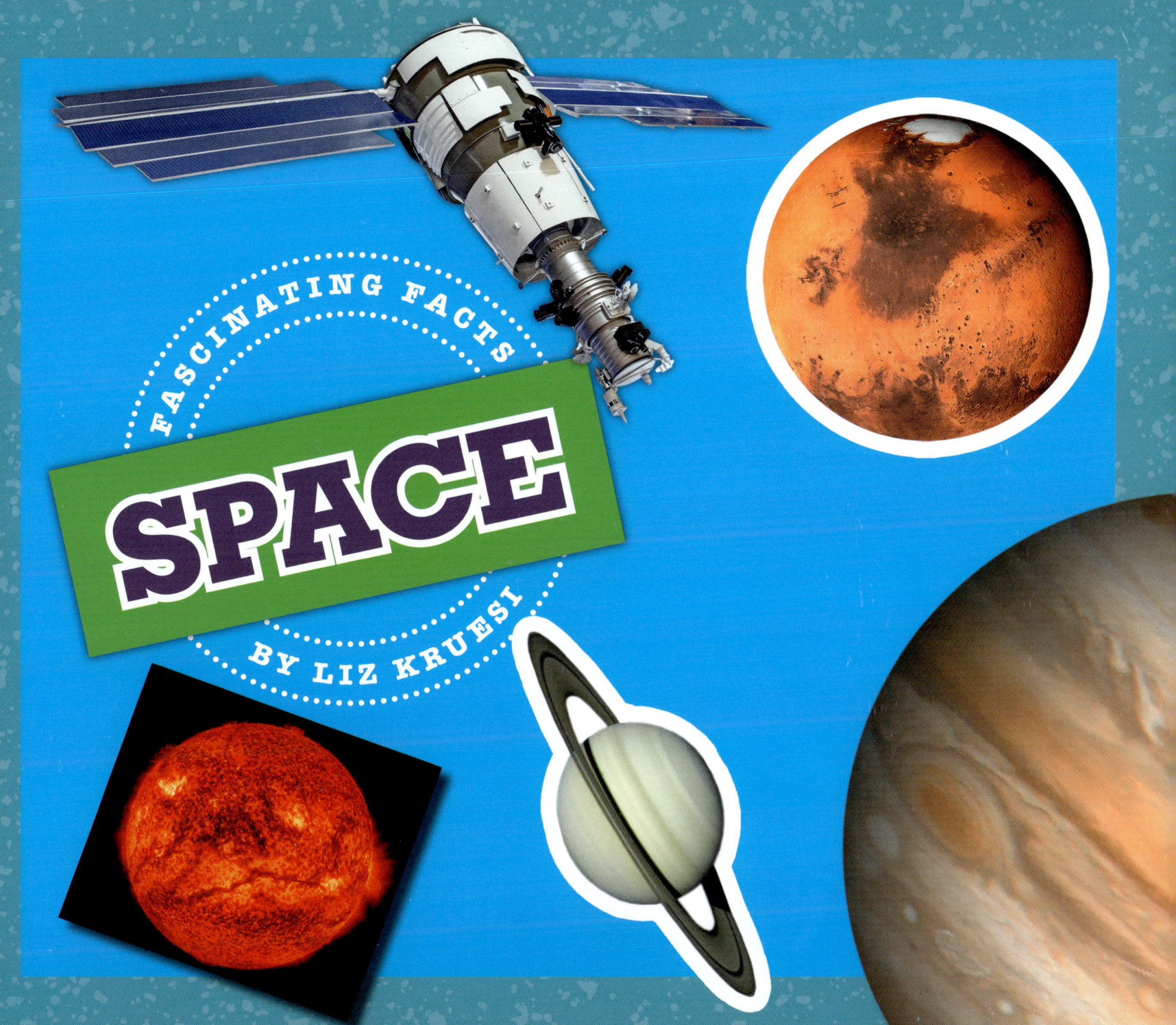

Published by The Child's World®
1980 Lookout Drive • Mankato, MN 56003-1705
800-599-READ • www.childsworld.com

Photographs ©: NASA, cover (sun), cover (Jupiter), cover (Saturn), 1 (sun), 1 (Jupiter), 1 (Saturn), 2, 7, 8, 9 (top), 10, 11 (left), 11 (right), 12, 13, 16, 18, 20, back cover (astronaut), back cover (Moon); Shutterstock Images, cover (satellite), cover (Mars), 1 (satellite), 1 (Mars), 3, 5 (right), 6, 14–15, 17, 19, 24; Pozdeyev Vitaly/Shutterstock Images, 4; iStockphoto, 5 (left); NASA Images/Shutterstock Images, 9 (bottom); Levent Konuk/Shutterstock Images, 15; Bill Chizek/Shutterstock Images, 21

Copyright © 2021 by The Child's World®
All rights reserved. No part of this book may be reproduced or utilized in any form or by any means without written permission from the publisher.

ISBN 9781503844636 (Reinforced Library Binding)
ISBN 9781503846319 (Portable Document Format)
ISBN 9781503847507 (Online Multi-user eBook)
LCCN 2019958003

Printed in the United States of America

ABOUT THE AUTHOR
Liz Kruesi lives in the Denver, Colorado, area. When she is not writing about science, she enjoys walking her dogs, hiking with her husband, and making jewelry.

CONTENTS

Introduction . . . 4

CHAPTER ONE
The Solar System . . . 6

CHAPTER TWO
Space Activities . . . 12

CHAPTER THREE
The Big Picture . . . 16

Glossary . . . 22

To Learn More . . . 23

Index . . . 24

INTRODUCTION

The next time you go outside at night, look above you into the dark sky. Out there are stars like the Sun. There are planets like Mars and Jupiter. There are huge groups of stars, called **galaxies**. All of this stuff is in the universe. And the universe is huge.

Scientists study the stars and planets to learn how they work. **Astronomers** investigate galaxies to see how they grow. They also can track how the universe changes. ▼

▲
There is still so much that scientists do not know. Many of the things they have discovered are fascinating. And there is still so much more to learn!

CHAPTER ONE

The Solar System

Mercury is the closest planet to the Sun, but it is not the hottest. That record goes to Venus. Venus has a thick, cloudy atmosphere that traps heat. There, it is 880 degrees Fahrenheit (471°C) and hot enough to melt metal.

Mars has the biggest canyon in the solar system. ▶ This area is as long as the United States is wide!

▶ The Moon does not make its own light. The Sun's light **reflects** off the surface of the Moon, just like light from a flashlight bounces off a mirror.

Mars used to have rivers and lakes of water. Scientists think those rivers raged for one or two billion years.

The Moon is moving away from Earth by 1.5 inches (3.8 cm) each year. The Earth spins a tiny bit slower because of this.

Gas Planets

Scientists think Saturn's rings will disappear in around ▶ 290 million years. The planet will look very different to future astronomers!

Three of Jupiter's moons, Europa, Callisto, and Ganymede, have underground lakes or oceans.

The four big planets in our solar system all have rings. Saturn's rings are very bright. Jupiter, Uranus, and Neptune have fainter rings.

An enormous storm bigger than all of Earth swirls on Jupiter. This is called the Giant Red Spot. It has churned for at least 150 years.

Over 100 jets of water shoot from the south pole of Saturn's moon Enceladus. This moon is believed to have an underground lake that feeds those plumes.

Uranus moves differently around the Sun than the other planets. It rolls on its side instead of spinning like a top.

Other Worlds

Both Pluto and the large, rocky asteroid Ceres have ice volcanoes on their surfaces. These do not spew hot lava like Earth's volcanoes. Instead, they spew a slushy ice mix.

A rocky object called Ceres is the biggest asteroid in the solar system. It sits in a ring of rocks between Mars and Jupiter. When Ceres was discovered in 1801, scientists incorrectly called it a planet because it was so huge.

Comets are small ice, gas, and dust balls that are found in the outer places of our solar system. Comets can have tails made of dust and **plasma**. These tails can be millions of miles long!

It takes Pluto 248 Earth-years to orbit the Sun. No one alive has been around long enough to see Pluto orbit the Sun once!

A robot visited Pluto for the first time in 2015. It took detailed pictures of Pluto and even found it has a thin atmosphere! The robot did all of this while running on less power than two light bulbs.

CHAPTER TWO

Space Activities

As of 2019, only 12 people have walked on the Moon. These were the Apollo **astronauts**. They visited the Moon between 1968 and 1972.

Astronauts from 19 countries ▶ have spent time on a huge space lab called the International Space Station. This lab is about the size of a football field. It has been in space for more than 20 years.

The astronauts that went to the Moon brought back 842 pounds (382 kg) of rocks and soil. These Moon pieces can be more expensive than diamonds. But, unlike diamonds, people cannot buy these Moon rocks.

To prepare for going to space, astronauts put on a special suit and practice moving in a huge swimming pool. Astronauts feel less **gravity** in space. It feels like floating in a pool.

The **rockets** that pushed the Apollo astronauts to the Moon were taller than the Statue of Liberty.

What Else Has Gone to Space?

Scientists track about 22,300 pieces of material ▶ around Earth. These are all made by humans. They are pieces of rockets, science experiments, and satellites.

Many animals have traveled to space. Scientists have sent spiders and bees to see if they could spin their webs or build their honeycombs with less gravity. Many years ago, monkeys and chimps went to space to show it was safe for human astronauts.

People know of only one animal that can survive in space without a suit or spaceship. This is called a tardigrade, or water bear. This creature is related to worms and centipedes, but it looks different. It is the size of a pencil point and has eight stubby legs.

▲
One experiment on the International Space Station found that fish swim in circles like the hands on a clock. That is because in space they lose their sense of balance.

CHAPTER THREE

The Big Picture

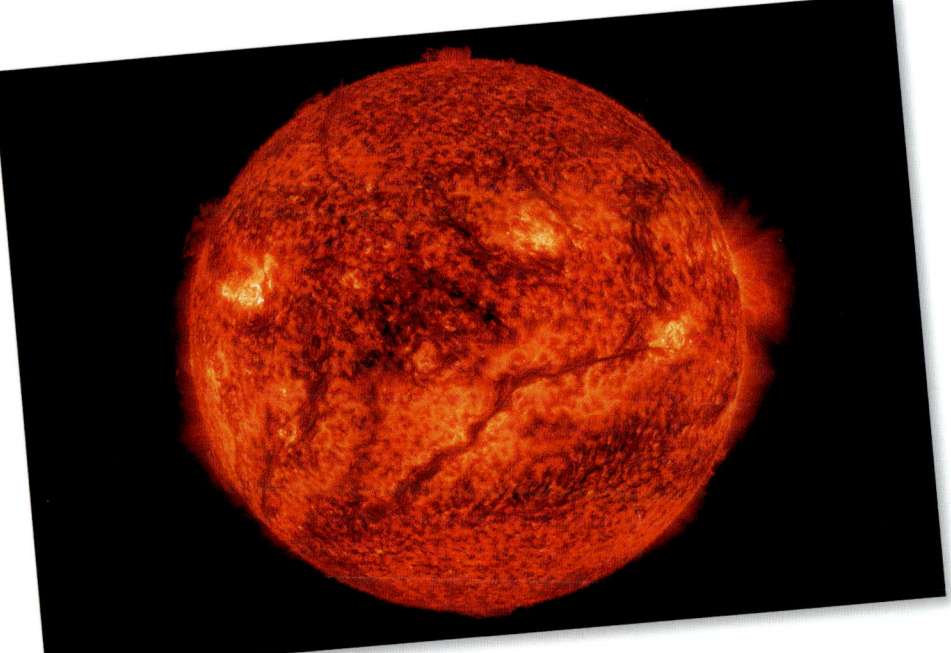

Our Sun is the only star ▶ in our solar system. The next nearest star to us is 25 trillion miles (40 trillion km) from the Sun.

Every star has at least one planet around it. These planets are called **exoplanets**. Some are made of gas like Jupiter, some are made of rock like Earth, and others do not look like anything in our solar system.

Stars can be yellow like our Sun. They can also be other colors, such as red, white, orange, or blue. The color of the star depends on how hot it is. Blue stars are hotter than red and orange ones.

Some types of stars spin very fast. The fastest star scientists have discovered makes 716 complete spins every second!

When a big star dies, it explodes. The explosion can be brighter than its whole galaxy.

Light takes many thousands of years to travel from the Sun's center to its ▲ surface. Then, it takes only eight minutes and 19 seconds to arrive at Earth!

Galaxies

Earth is in the Milky Way galaxy. Our galaxy has a spiral pinwheel shape. Our solar system is about halfway between the center of the pinwheel and the edge.

▲ A galaxy is a group of stars, gas, and dust. The universe has billions of them. There are so many galaxies that if you look through a straw, thousands of galaxies would fill that tiny hole. You cannot see them with your eye, though. They are far away, and their light is very faint.

Humans can see only one kind of light. We call this visible light. But there are many other types of light that nature produces. If you could see other types of light, you would see enormous bubbles at the center of our galaxy.

Almost every galaxy has ▲ something called a **black hole** at its center. A black hole has so much gravity that it pulls in anything that gets too close—including light!

The Universe

Space is really cold! It is -455 degrees Fahrenheit (-270°C). That is about 3 degrees above the coldest temperature possible.

Scientists say there are billions of ghostlike particles that travel through people every second. These particles carry energy. They come from the Sun and many other cosmic objects and are called neutrinos.

Light from other galaxies takes millions of years to reach Earth. Because of that, scientists with powerful telescopes see these galaxies as they were millions of years ago.

Astronomers think there could be a **multiverse**. This means there might be many other universes, some like ours and some not.

All the stars, planets, life, galaxies, and space dust make up only 5 percent of the universe. The other 95 percent is mysterious and invisible. Scientists do not know how to see it. But they know it is there because the stars and galaxies move in surprising ways.

Glossary

astronauts (AS-truh-nots) Astronauts are people who have been to space. The first astronauts traveled to space in 1961.

astronomers (as-TRON-uh-merz) Astronomers are people who study space and the universe. Astronomers discover new things about the universe.

black hole (BLAK HOLE) A black hole is a space that has infinitely strong gravity. When a star explodes, a black hole is formed.

exoplanets (EK-soh-plan-ets) Exoplanets are round and big objects that orbit a star. Scientists have found thousands of exoplanets.

galaxies (GAL-ak-seez) Galaxies are systems of stars held together by gravity. The Milky Way is one of many galaxies.

gravity (GRAV-i-tee) Gravity is the force that pulls an object of less mass toward an object of more mass. Space has less gravity than Earth.

multiverse (MULL-tee-verse) A multiverse is many universes at the same time, each one filled with space and material. Math equations show our universe may be a small part of the multiverse.

plasma (PLAZ-ma) Plasma is a gas that has a lot of energy added to it. The Sun is made of plasma.

reflects (ree-FLEKTS) Something that reflects bounces light and changes its direction. Sunlight reflects off a lake's surface.

rockets (ROK-etts) Rockets are objects that use an explosion to fire another object into space. In the United States, rockets launch mostly from Florida.

To Learn More

In the Library

Nichols, Michelle. *Astronomy Lab for Kids: 52 Family-Friendly Activities*. Beverly, MA: Quarry, 2016.

Ringstad, Arnold. *The International Space Station*. Mankato, MN: The Child's World, 2016.

Stone, Jerry. *Space Travel*. New York, NY: DK Publishing, 2019.

On the Web

Visit our website for links about space:
childsworld.com/links

Note to Parents, Teachers, and Librarians: We routinely verify our Web links to make sure they are safe and active sites. So encourage your readers to check them out!

Index

animals, 14–15
astronauts, 12–14
astronomers, 5, 8, 21

black hole, 19

Ceres, 10
comets, 11

Earth, 7, 9–11, 14, 16–17, 18, 21
exoplanets, 16

galaxies, 4–5, 17–19, 21

International Space Station, 13, 15

Jupiter, 4, 8–10, 16

Mars, 4, 6–7, 10
Mercury, 6
moons, 7–8, 9, 12–13

Neptune, 8

Pluto, 10–11

Saturn, 8–9
stars, 4–5, 16–17, 18, 21
Sun, 4, 6–7, 9, 11, 16–17, 20

Uranus, 8–9

Venus, 6